Winter Park Library

Songs from the Land of Dawn

Songs from the Land of Dawn

by
TOYOHIKO KAGAWA
and other Japanese Poets

•

INTERPRETATION BY
LOIS J. ERICKSON

•

DECORATIONS BY
HENRY Y. SUGIMOTO

Friendship Press • New York

MANUFACTURED IN THE UNITED STATES OF AMERICA

First Printing May 1949
Second Printing May 1956

895.61
Son

TO
ROBERT AND ELAINE
FRANK, LOIS, ALEX JUNIOR, AND ETHEL

Acknowledgment

The translator wishes to acknowledge her indebtedness
to Mr. Masato Ishibashi and other Japanese
friends in Hamilton, Ontario, for the
invaluable help they have given her.

Introduction

*D*URING the war we of America wondered what Kagawa was thinking, feeling, saying. Through the confusion came echoes and reports, but no clear word. We knew that wherever Kagawa was, the Christian conscience was searchingly at work. How did the other side of war's iron curtain look to one who had lived on the Calvary side of life? Would the atom bomb silence the ambassador of love whose words had been a living link between Japan and America?

Now we know. The message of Kagawa has not been stilled. In these poems its essence has been distilled. Here it is:

> Jesus is not dead;
> Still as of old,
> He seeks his sheep.

How could a Kagawa convey the feelings that were bursting through his breaking heart? When thoughts "break through language and escape," poetry and the arts come the nearest to catching them. The prophet and the poet are co-workers in spiritual creation. The former sees the vision; the latter, as Shelley said, preserves from decay the visitation of divinity. At their best, prophecy and poetry blend. Such a union is found in Toyohiko Kagawa.

For the making of peace, imagination is needed even more than information. World outlooks must be transformed into world sympathies. Racial and national "problems" must become fellowship projects. This is the task of the church, the prophet, the poet. This is the achievement of Kagawa.

His lines leave images that sear the brain—babies on backs of horror-stricken refugees, impoverished passengers propped in the washrooms of trains, "God's poor children, lost, afraid," "dumb in defeat, struggling to live." If it be true that "our sweetest strains are those which speak of saddest thought," Kagawa's verse might have sufficient value in the mere fact of its poignant beauty. But through the shadows that hang so heavy over his beloved land plays the light of the prophet's undimmed faith. It is dawn, not dusk, that he depicts.

These little poems are the current epistles of a contemporary Saint Paul. Here we see the scars of the body becoming the badge of spiritual victory. Here we see a soul coming "more than conqueror" through tribulation, nakedness, peril, the sword. Kagawa gives us a glimpse behind the curtain of the past few years and it is dark; he also gives us a glimpse "behind the beyond" and it is light.

Worthy to rank with Kagawa's work are the poems of his contemporary Christians. They, too, found songs to express the experience of coming up out of great tribulation.

The classical *haiku* of ancient Japan provide revealing glimpses of a people's thought life. With great sensitivity Mrs. Erickson conveys to us Japan's exquisite appreciation of beauty. This experience will make many of us contritely revise our opinion of Japanese character.

RALPH W. SOCKMAN

Christ Methodist Church
New York

Contents

PART THREE ❦ SELECTED CLASSICAL POEMS

Part One

POEMS BY KAGAWA

Interpreter's Foreword

Unloved and lonely here I sit
Leaning against my brazier;
Now and then I raise myself
To rake dead ashes.

God, how I long for Thee!
All feeling else is gone,
This three-mat hole
Where sunlight never strikes,
This poverty so dread
That I would fain
Cast out the cat I cannot feed.
(The cat that comes again and yet again)—

But I am satisfied, satisfied . . .
My eyes behold Thee here,
And when I close them
I can feel Thee watching
By my side.

Farewell to paper pasted walls;
I get me up
And shove my shoddy sandals on.
Throughout this land I go to preach,
"The Kingdom is at hand!"

So wrote young Kagawa in his diary-in-verse, *Songs from the Slums*. His concern at that time was for individuals in the terrible place where he lived for over fourteen years: the homeless who slept with him on the broken floor of his tiny room; murderers who attacked him; the boy whose father kicked him naked into the streets; the idiot woman dying of plague; his little "girl disciple" who was sold.

This frail student used to preach to the factory workers going out in the dark winter mornings to their long days of toil. He dreamed of better things, and went to prison for organizing the first labor union. Social service on a vast scale was developed through the years—co-operatives for city workers and peasants; homes for ex-prisoners, for tubercular patients, and for lepers; orphanages, hospitals. Kagawa has written more than sixty books. And he has remained a Christian pastor.

In 1940, Dr. Kagawa was imprisoned for opposing the war with China. Hard things were said of him during World War II. The police announced that he had given up Christianity, and that he had toured the Philippines spreading propaganda. Instead, though bitterly persecuted, he was continuing to preach. But he had to be careful, lest he bring disaster upon all Christians. Before our soldiers came ashore after the surrender, Kagawa was organizing a National Repentance Society. When invited to become premier of Japan, he replied in the spirit of forty years ago, "Throughout the land I go to preach!"

He is now "traveling ceaselessly proclaiming God." No longer is there time to nurse one starving baby back to life. But his influence reaches millions. He frequently contributes a column of prose-poetry to the great *Asahi Newspaper,* and it is from these poems that we quote.

Prelude

I have seen beauty —
Flaming clouds at sunset;
Seas dyed to scarlet as
  the night comes on;
Bowers of flowers mirrored
  in the lakelets;
Grandeur of gorges;
  Fuji in the dawn!

Lacy green trees outlined in misty
    vistas
Suddenly lighted by a flare of maple
    leaves;
Far below the mountaintop the ripen-
    ing rice fields waving
'Round little brown mud hovels with
    straw-thatched eaves.

Now War and Death have come to you,
  O lovely Land of Morning,
Dull despair of sorrow and bitter-
    ness of pain;
God grant us both forgiveness for the
    wrongs we did each other;—
Out of deep hatred bring us Love again!

Lois J. Erickson

O SKYLARKS, TEACH JAPAN TO SING

Night skies grow white
And larks fly up
And sing to wake the dawn.

Brave little birds,
I saw you
Spring from the wheat fields
When the cannon ceased to roar,
And spread your wings
And sing
Your hymns to God.

Over the rushing crowds,
Seeking a refuge
From the cruel bombs,
You sang to comfort
God's poor children,
Lost, afraid.

And now defeat
Has come.
Men have forgotten
How to sing;
But larks
Do not forget.

They are such little things,
And yet with mighty voices
They sing songs
That shake the sky—
Bright songs of adoration
For their God.

Oh, I have heard them sing
In many lands;
And as I listened
I have stood and prayed
Until the music ceased.

On cloudy days
They sing
After the rain is gone
And winds are calm,
In summer skies
They sing,
So blithely that they almost burst
Their little hearts!
And as I hear,
I pity this poor land
That has forgotten song.

O larks,
Teach us to sing again;
Oh, teach Japan
To sing to God!

THE KINGDOM OF GOD
IS WITHIN YOU

Chaos in all the world;
In Japan
Defeat . . . .
Poverty . . . .
Utter destitution . . . .
Yet there is also love
That gives and shares,
Thankfulness,
Sacrifice,
And silent uncomplaint.

For where the Spirit of the Cross
Shines deep
Within their hearts,
God's saints
Await the Day of Glory,
And his Kingdom
Has already come.

Except in holy love
Where can we look for
Heaven?
For Heaven is more than just a place;
It is a state of soul,
A living with our God,
And knowing
He is everywhere.

Heaven is
The Spirit of the Cross,
By which,
Forgiving and forgiven,
One loves all — suffers all.

The Kingdom
Has already come
To this world
Through the Cross;
And Christ's disciples,
Living in His life
      Bring Light.

Light even to
The shacks destroyed by war;
And to the land laid low
By storm and earthquake.
So to him who cries,
"Japan is ruined!" I would say,
"You must forget your *Self,*
And you must learn to love!"

For lo,
The Kingdom is
Not here, nor there;
The Kingdom is
Within the soul,
Not to be seen,
But felt.

Yes, verily, I know
That only through the Kingdom
There will some day come
The resurrection of Japan.

WAITING FOR DAWN

Hurrying on my trip,
I leave my home
And hasten to the station,
The morning star
Still shining
In the winter sky.

I board the train,
And as I watch,
Dark blue is turned to azure,
Azure then to green:
I feel my heart
Is being cleansed
In this brief moment
Just before the dawn.

Green turns to gold;
Bright beams shoot toward the clouds;
I travel to the east
To welcome sunrise;
Yet the colors are
So wonderful,
It seems too bad
That they must vanish
With the mounting sun.

Oh, I have prayed
Through many a night
For this poor rabble
That is now Japan.
Eight months
I traveled ceaselessly,
Proclaiming God.

For fifty nights
I rode in third class cars;
[Broken cars,

Jolting over broken railways;
So full
That passengers
Crawled through,
Were pushed through,
Pulled through
Broken windows;
Cold in winter,
Stifling hot
In summer;
Choked by the smoke
Of countless tunnels;
Crowded so close
That aisles were packed with people;
Babies on backs;
Tired children crying;
Men propped on washbowls;
People sitting
Even upon the evil-smelling floor.*]

I am waiting
For the sunrise
In my country,
For the bright beginning
Of a new Japan . . . .
As Israel waited for its heart's desire,
Lead us again, O God, by cloud and fire.

*Details of postwar travel included inside brackets were taken from a
letter written to the interpreter by a missionary friend.

SPRING

Spring has come back again
With white trees blossoming,
And warmth of waters flowing;
Yet in men's hearts is lingering
Cold sorrow of defeat.

You who were bold and brave
In plundering,
Falter not now, but face
Your mightier task,
And build Japan again!

O Youth of Sunrise Land,
Almighty God would use
This cruel war

To teach and train you; —
If you fail to learn
His lessons,
You will prove yourselves
Unworthy to be called
The sons of dawn.

Dark though this bitter night,
Day will be bright with light;
Tears disappear,
When God Eternal shines
Upon your minds.
He sends the warmth of spring,
This time of blossoming;
Then sing,
O Spirit of Japan,
Then sing!

MIRRORS

For more than twenty years,
My clouded eyes
Have been too weak
To look into a glittering mirror.

So does a clouded conscience
Suffer,
When it would behold
The glory of God's face.

THE LIVING CHRIST

Paul was the only man
Who ever saw our Lord
After His entrance
Into Heaven
To dwell with God.

Paul met Him
On the rough Damascus Road.
And from that time
Christ dwelt in Paul,
Giving him help,
Comfort in sickness,
And in persecution, strength —
Christ was his whole existence.

So to us
Today
Christ gives eternal life, —

He Who was crucified,
And triumphed,
Through the Power of Love.
Our Lord is in our hearts
And flesh and blood,
Helping us always.

Why should we speak
Of "Christianity"
As though it were
Dead doctrine?
Jesus is not dead;
Still as of old,
He seeks His sheep.

The Christ is everywhere:—
The lepers find Him
In their dark despair;
He shines in the grey dawn
Beyond the dungeon bars;
And by our death beds
He is there!

Children of Japan,
Dumb in defeat,
Struggling to live,
Wipe, wipe away your tears,
Look at the living Christ;
   He stands
   Here at your side.

ONE WITH THE UNIVERSE

To do a thing alone is difficult;
Easy, when men work together.
A sage once said,
"The wise man works through others";
But the best of all
Is that we trust
Our work to God.

Man cannot do the work of ants or bees,
Nor of the ocean creatures.
Yet I know
That man and beast are brothers;
And the ant's absorbing work is mine.
So, too, with life
Of bird and fish;
And through this kinship,
I can feel that I am one
With all the universe.

My fancy then can make me one
With plant or rock,
Bearing me far
From cheats and liars,
Out to a mountain meadow,
And I can become
A sweet blue cornflower,
Looking up
Into the sun.

Nature is life and art to me —
I need no paint nor canvas,
Marble, nor a harp,
Because I have
Harmony in my soul.

This earth is wide;
The world of human beings
Not the only world for me;
God made
His creatures wonderful,
And I am one
With all His universe.

JAPAN CAN TEACH

The world would be the better for
Two lessons
That Japan can teach:—

The purity of beauty
In simplicity:

The loyalty
And chivalry of each to each
Which make our country
One great family.

(A condensation)

THE SIMPLE LIFE

Perhaps one would be better off
If one were dead;
But since we are alive
And know defeat,
Better than wilful chatter,
Better than selfish struggle
For the means to eat,
Let us serve God and man,
And *give* —
That is the way to live!

I like the simple life;
I'm sixty,
But I've never had
A best suit yet;
When there is need
The doctor close at hand
Has one that I can get.

There is convenience
In the simple life;
I find it good,
And practise commonness
In clothing, home, and food.
It is a pleasure
Not to be burdened
With too much of treasure!

The reindeer's horns
Are big and very tall;
But when he has to fight
They cause his fall.
To very wealthy men
Misfortunes come.
A suit case in each hand,
One cannot run.

If you have always lived
    In luxury,
It would be very sad to drop
    To poverty,

And misery,
But even prison does not seem too bad,
If you have only known
    Simplicity.
I had been living long
In Kobe slum,
So I was not dismayed
To have policemen come;
After the tiny huts on every hand,
Even the prison then seemed very grand!

You who are left with nothing,
Remember Jesus said,
"The Son of Man hath nowhere
On the earth to lay His head."

I CALL THE SWALLOWS

Swallows,
Swallows,
Come back,
For Spring is here;
Over oceans,
Over mountains,
Little mates together,
In the warm Spring weather;

Do you laugh at Man —
At his foolish warships,
At his atom bombs,
At his drunken sleep?
Do you laugh
Because he digs
His own grave
   Deep?

When I was a child
Down in the land of Awa,
I wondered that the swallows,
Year after year,
Came back to their same nests again;
Just as Jeremiah wondered
At God's guidance of the swallows,
And wept,
As he thundered,

"My people Israel
Will not return!"

Christ said,
"Behold the fowls
Of the air—
They sow not,
They reap not,
Nor gather into barns:
And yet,
Your Heavenly Father
Feedeth them."

O brothers,
Coming back
Empty handed,
Desolate,
From your sojourn
Beyond the seven seas,
Look up,
Behold the birds . . . .
And are ye not much better
Than are these?

SILENCE

In times of quietness
Our hearts should be like trees,
Lifting their branches to the sky
To draw down strength
Which they will need
To face storms that will surely come.

The still earth
Takes its own majestic way;
The quiet heavens declare
God's glory.
Christ said nothing
As he moved
From Pilate's judgment seat
To Calvary.

The stars are silent,
Flowers do not sing;
But stars fill all the night
With light more beautiful than sound.
Flowers are bright with color
Lovelier than song.
God's blessings
Fall upon us wordlessly,
Eternal as the quiet passing
Of the sun.

Why should we fear?

His silent presence
Will be with us
Till the end;
His hand at last
Will lay us tenderly away
When life is past.

WORK

I shall not say
That I am busy:—
Those who would help
The troubled people
Should expect to be
Busy always.

Christ was so thronged
By multitudes
He had no time to eat.
He said,
"To him that hath
Shall be given;
And from him that hath not
Shall be taken away
Even that
He seems to have."
Which means
That if we do not use

All of our powers
We lose them.

This also
We must not forget —
System, which gets work done!
Then, too, the problem is
To do our work
With all our hearts;
We do not tire
Of doing what we love.

But most of all,
Our strength and comfort come
Only when God
Dwells in our souls
Working together with us.

LOVE MEANS ADVENTURE

Not fighting only —
Love, too, means
Adventure.

Nurses go bravely forth to nurse
Cases that may mean death;
Firemen do not flee
The raging flames;
To save ex-convicts
You yourself
Face danger at their hands.

Fuji Ishii
Fasted and prayed
For ten long years
To feed his orphans.
Yamamuro sacrificed
Both wife and children
In his fight
To save the world.

There have been many martyrs:—
David Livingstone
Died on his knees
In darkest Africa;
Williams was devoured
By cannibals
In the New Hebrides . . . .
Jesus went out to die
On Calvary.

Peace means adventure, too.
On the day
That war was over,
Yet another war
For Love and Peace began.

Unrest is seething;
We can not
Sit idly by;
Courage is needed,
Fresh and vigorous.

Without the Spirit of the Cross
Japan can not be saved.
Give up the thought
Of wealth and honors;
Struggle desperately
Against all hazards,
Even death.
Remembering that

The Campaign of the Crucifixion
Means adventure,
Now and always.
Remembering
That from this campaign
There will come
The light of peace
And happiness
To sad Japan.

Let every one of us
Rush gladly in,
And brave the wildness
Of the awful storm!

CHRIST LIVETH IN ME

"That Christ may dwell
Within your hearts
By faith,"
Thus did Paul write
To friends in Ephesus.

For Christ to Paul
Was not a Being
To be worshiped from afar,
But One Who dwelt within.

When Thought Police
Threw me in jail,
(For Jesus' sake)
I sat two days and nights
Upon the prison floor,
My head upon my knees,
Discouraged, miserable,
And prayed.

And then the vision came —
I had been seeking for the Christ
Too far away;
But now I saw
That He could live in me!

Live with me always —
In the night
Came comfort,
For I tried to feel
That He was there,
And in the morning
That His love
Awaited me.

Then as I paced the prison grounds
He walked with me;
And as I read the books allowed
(The books on science),
Then He talked with me,
And made me know

That real truth is of God;
Shimbashi Prison thus became
      God's temple!

For from the very moment
When my vision came,
My tears were gone
And all my fears were gone.

Christ was with me
As I faced examination
By the fierce police;
And He was there
When I was brought
Before the judge,
Expecting death,
And praying that I might not shame
The Christ within my heart.

Christ, Who didst walk on Galilee,
Lead me to peace in this sad world;
Thou Who didst fall asleep in that frail boat
      On storm-tossed sea,
Oh, lead me to that world where all is understood—
      Live Thou, O Christ, in me!

Part Two

SELECTED CHRISTIAN POEMS

Interpreter's Foreword

JAPANESE love art and poetry. Both are manly accomplishments. Each New Year the Emperor announces the subject of the annual poetry contest, and leads off with his own composition. Most cultured Japanese have at some time attempted verselets in the ancient classical style. However, the prose poem, as written by Dr. Kagawa and the Yamamuros, is becoming popular, and Christian hymns are being written in the strict meters of the West.

There is on a tiny islet of the Inland Sea called Oshima a government hospital for victims of leprosy. For thirty-five years my husband had a part in the Christian work being done for these people. The first patient admitted was Honami Nagata, a young student with poetry in his soul. He was won from suicidal despair by the Bible teaching, "Neither did this man sin, nor his parents, but that the works of God be made manifest." Until his death more than thirty years later, Nagata was one of the leaders of the church. He was the organizer of the Poetry Club of Oshima.

Among the members were Kanda, whose wife's people had again and again stolen her away from him because of his disease; Yamamoto, who had been a teacher of English; Takamoto, gentle and resigned in his blindness; Miyoshi, whose face shone with heavenly light as he sang. There were Mr. and Mrs. Miyauchi, terribly afflicted, but both gifted in the expression of their faith. There was Susumu Fujita, one of the boy twins who "prayed like preachers." There was Miyake San, head of the Christian community. And there were many others. Quite a number of the poems in Part Two have appeared in *Hearts Aglow* and other publications of the American Mission to Lepers. Permission has been given us to make these available to a wider circle of readers.

Utako Hayashi was an early convert to Christianity. While still very young, she founded an orphanage on such slender resources that at one time she had to feed her children for two days on five cents worth of potatoes, bought on credit. After many years of fine Christian service, she became president of the W.C.T.U. and a leading fighter for peace, purity, and prohibition.

Takayoshi Matsuyama did his greatest work as one of the translators of the Bible. On his death at eighty-eight, the verse we use was engraved in Japanese on a beautiful bronze vase presented by his family to the British and Foreign Bible Society in London.

Back in the 1860's Gumpei Yamamuro was born to a mother who prayed Buddha to make her son a great and good man. Grown to youth, this boy was one day handed a Christian tract. Curiosity aroused, he sought out a church. Very soon he asked for baptism. But the minister thought him unprepared and unprepossessing. Gumpei's heart was broken. One summer afternoon when rain was falling, he climbed to the roof, slipped out of his ragged clothes, and prayed, "O God, I trust in Christ for salvation. Baptize Thou me in this pure water of heaven!" The whole thrilling story cannot be told here. Later Yamamuro joined the Salvation Army, and for many years was its commissioner. His daughter Tamiko, whose poems we quote, is also active in the work of the Salvation Army.

IN ALL THINGS, VICTORY

He hears me pray to Him upon the deep,
When masts are gone, and tattered sails are blown
By storms that drive my frail boat out to sea;
He hears, and sends the wind that wafts me home.

Naught that can come shall bring despair to me,
Gaining in all things more than victory!

He hears me pray to Him when I am lost
Amid wild mountains, and no path can see;
He saves me from the beasts and from the night,
And gives the comfort of His strength to me.

He hears me pray to Him when my tired feet
Struggle across the desert's burning sand;
With His own blood restores my fainting soul,
And to green pastures leads me by the hand.

The limits of the earth are wide and vast,
And vaster still its smiling dome of blue,
Yet through this space I always hear His voice,
"O little one," He says, "I died for you!"

My Lord in me has found a dwelling place,
And I in Him. Oh, glorious boon to gain
To be His temple! Gladly will I face,
In His great strength, all bitterness and pain!

Nagata

MORNING PRAYER

I waken in the early dawn
    And softly pray
That I may find and do the work
    God has for me this day.

               Utako Hayashi

A lowly woman,
    Singing in her heart,
Stoops to draw water for her heavy jar,
    While in the sky
A bright moon lights the dawn.

               Utako Hayashi

A SONG OF DAILY LIFE

Again today, Lord,
    Let me write
In characters of sweat and tears
    Words that will bring
    Thy children to the light.

And faith and hope and love
    Will be
The warp and woof
Of fabric gay
    That I would weave for Thee
        Today.

               Utako Hayashi

THE NEW YEAR

The year
An uncut jewel is,
Of matchless worth;
Bringing along with it
New heaven and earth;
I long to dwell with God,
Oh, through this year,
Blessed with His blessing
    May I live
    A life of prayer!

Tsurue Miyauchi

GOD'S PLAN

God planned
The little grain of sand
I hold upon my hand,
And so it need not be
Hard for my faith to see
    He plans for me!

Miyoshi

THE THOUGHT OF GOD

To me
The thought of God
Is this —

The first step
In my daily life.
Of all importance,
For I leave this earth
To enter Heaven,
All things else forgot,
All disappointment wiped away.

Unworthy though I am,
The thought of God
Is this —
Deep prayer
That is a well of shining hope,
And strength, and happiness.

It is a time when bounteous manna falls;
A time I learn the mysteries of the Word;
A time I breathe the breath of life,
And bathe my soul in God.

It is a time
When I see Heaven as my home;
The time I meet the Risen Christ!

Nagata

HIS WILL

I would not change one little jot
  Of His dear will for me;
But in my weakness I would go
Entrusting all my load of woe
  To Him Who walks with me.

Kanda

THE THORN

When I would pray,
"Lord take the thorn away,"
Clearly there comes to me
  A vision of His Cross!

Mumei (Anonymous)

GETHSEMANE

I sit alone and silent,
And deep thoughts come to me
About a little garden on a hill —
Gethsemane!

"A Believer"

LOOKING UP

We that are sick
Must suffer pain,
Yes, that may be —
But this our comfort,
That it leaves us free
To look up quietly
    At Calvary.

Hiromi

DAWN

At dawn the reading of the Word
Its daily message brings,
And all the while a bonnie bird
Beside my window sings;
And when I wander to the shore
To kneel beside the sea,
From out the pine-grove on the hill
The birds still sing to me.

Tanikado

MY TASK

At morn to kneel before Him,
In the night to pray
For happiness of all men
    Every day —
This the task I love.

Hayashi

MY ROAD

Pierce through my heart,
O message of the cross,
That I may know
That way that leads among the thorns must be
The road I go!

Handa

A CHILD OF PRAYER

This is the blessing
That I ask of Thee —
Weakness made strong:
That I may be
A child of prayer,
Burning for Thee.

Mumei

LEADING

I do not fear to tread the path
I cannot see
Because the hand of One-Who-Loves,
Is leading me.

Nagata

PRAYER REACHES HIM

Strive though it may, no power in earth or sky
Can move the Spirit of the Lord Most High;
What reaches Him upon His mighty throne
Is prayer alone.

Nagata

THOU ART

I know *Thou art*
When sudden prayer
Wells all unbidden
In my humble heart.

Kawabuchi

PRAYER

Oh, make my heart so still, so still,
    When I am deep in prayer,
That I might hear the white mist-wreaths
    Losing themselves in air!

Utsunomiya

BOTH ARE BLESSING

All joy is God's own gift,
    All suffering,
    And both are blessing
So I shall give thanks
    In everything!

Egi

TRUE LOVE

If true love is there,
The more we love
Then all the more we pray;
There is no greater love than prayer.

Mumei

MY ALL

He adds each day grace unto grace,
Unfolding love is in His face,
His joy abounds in every place,
    My Father is my All!

Takamoto

SUNSET

Upon the road which I have trod so long
Across the endless plain,
Sunset has come at last.

Mumei

HEAVEN

I live in light and love,
By God's grace given;
Yet is my hungry heart
Homesick for Heaven!

Takamoto

[38]

COMFORT

I rise before the dawn has come
        And go
     To pray apart;
And there the perfume of the flowering plum
   Comforts my lonely heart.

Miyauchi

YOUR DEATH

Like the glorious red of the sunrise
Like the shout at the battle's end,
The opening of gates into Heaven —
That was your death, O friend!

Takamoto

HIS GRACE

I hear His low voice say to me,
"Ever my grace sufficeth thee,"
   And I am glad.

Ishii

THANK THEE

One very earnest prayer is mine today —
The same that was so sweet on yesterday —
"Thank Thee, O Father!" This is what I say.

Egi

MY TREASURE

You ask my dearest treasure, and I come confessing
It is the burden God has turned to blessing!

Egi

GOD'S JUSTICE

Ah, those who love not God
Will find their doom far in the future years;
But He Whose justice sends them out from Him
    Will part from them with tears!

Nagata

SUNSHINE

If I should dwell now on the pain
Of soul and body that have come to me,
Nor heeding sunshine, look upon the rain,
How foolish, foolish my poor heart would be!

Fujita

THE SOUL LIKE IRON

The soul is like to iron
    Melted in the forge;
Each blow that strikes upon it
Makes it yet more strong!

Mumei

TO ONE IN HEAVEN

O You, with whom I used to learn of God,
How can I tell you how alone I am?
Your voice is in the lapping of the waves,
And in the wind's harp singing in the pines;
Night skies, white clouds, pale moonlight bring you
  near.
    But you are gone,
    And I am all alone . . . .

Let me not think of you
With bitterness in my hurt human heart,
But joyfully, because your faith
Has borne you up to God.

Come, heavenly mansions Jesus has prepared!
Come, glory at the Heavenly Father's feet!
   Some day . . . Some day . . . I, too.
   Pray for me;
   Wait for me. . . .
        Nagata

EASTER

Like snowflakes, or like petals of sweet flowers,
    In shining showers from Heaven,
My Father's promises to my full heart
    This Easter morn are given!

Miyoshi

NEW YEAR

The lovely light of stars
    Shines quietly
Where sleep the flowers
    Peacefully,
Before the New Year's dawn.
    I leave the past
    Determinedly,
    To face the future
    Manfully,
And bear my hard cross on!

Fujita

MY FLOWERS

'Twould be too bad to keep my flowers
All to myself;
So I shall lend
The precious vase
For one day
To a friend.

Shizumoki

AZALEAS

It seems to me that I can almost taste
The beauty of these wild azaleas,
Foaming along the hills!

Muda

THOUGHTFULNESS

I sat upon my little porch
And whiled the sunny hours;
A friend came by and stopped to let
Me smell his bunch of flowers!

Yamaguchi

LOVELINESS

To my sick eyes
One bit of loveliness lights up the gloom—
An oleander blooming by the window of my room.

Mumei

MY VIOLETS

My hands are numb and broken,
        I am blind;
And I can neither feel nor see
    My little bowl of violets,
    So I bend to kiss
    The wee, sweet flowers
    That mean so much to me.

Mumei

CHRYSANTHEMUMS

The color of my life,
Suffering and lonely for a score of years
Is that of little pale chrysanthemums
Grown wild upon the hills.

Mumei

THE MOON AND THE DEWDROP

The moon between the clouds shines down
Upon the little drop of dew
Dotting the tip of wayside grass,
And mirrors there its radiance.

Mumei

NOT ALONE

Flowers dead, friends gone,
An autumn night apart;
But not alone while prayer
Wells joyful in my heart!

Hayashi

GLORYING

The seasons pass;
Winter and summer, autumn and the spring;
But all the days in Christ's unchanging grace
I shall go glorying!

Miyauchi

LOTUS

Night showers cleared at dawn;
A little shining pond;
And the faint sound
Of lotus bursting into bloom!

Mumei

THE GOODNESS OF GOD

The fragrance of the trees,
The songs of birds,
The blossoming flowers
'Mid the mountain grasses,
All whisper to the soul
That waits to hear,
Saying, "God passes."
The treasures of the sea,
The fruits of fields,
These also praise;
The village smoke confesses,
As heavenward its columns
    Slowly rise,
"'Tis God that blesses!"

Nagata

SURPRISE

Above our isle,
A bank of scarlet clouds;
Upon the sea,
Where I was not expecting it,
A pale new moon!

Mumei

LOVELY THINGS

Those joys are very few
That illness brings;
So I shall lie and think
Of lovely things!

Mumei

AUTUMN

The rain has washed the sadness from the sky,
And clear and pure its beauty stretches high;
Athwart the east a great torch burns its way
In promise of a radiant autumn day.
But sorrow settles on the passing hours
And drives me to my brazier-side again
To listen to the sodden beat of rain
While cold wind rattles at the paper doors.
    Across the room
One perfect red flower blazes through the gloom.

Nagata

THE CARPENTER

Long, long ago
Beside a little grass-grown street
Of Nazareth,
Within a quiet shop,
He bent to plane tough boards
And saw hard wood,
While sweat dropped from His brow —
Our Lord and Master
In the form of man,
Who showed us thus
The worth of labor.

His salvation comes
Not from man's wisdom
Nor the lore of books,
But to those born again,
Whose hearts are made anew,
Be they but toilers, traders,
Peasants, poorest of the poor.

The grace of God
Is never limited

To men in gorgeous robes,
Who dwell in jeweled towers;
But He abides
Beside the hearths of hovels,
Where at morn and night
His children kneel
To lift their hearts to Him.

In faith then,
Let us pull the heavy wheels;
And in the Spirit
Draw the water
For our paddy fields,
Remembering that long ago
Jesus of Nazareth
Daily carved His wood,
And planed His long, hard boards.
So let us hold
His will for us
Deep in our hearts,
And labor on and on.

Gumpei Yamamuro

THE HILLS OF GOD

Why should my daily pathway seem
A desert stark and dry,
When all around the hills of God
Are glorious in the sky?

Takamoto

SO COLD

We set up tents,
Spread tables
For the day
Three thousand men and women,
Boys and girls,
Would come to us
To spend in play.
The children crowded in,
Shouting and pushing,
Scrambling for a place
Where they might eat
Their steaming bean-soup
Made with dumplings.

At evening when the fun was done
They saw us putting out
The kitchen fires,
And swarmed about us begging coals —
So many that we could not think
To count them.
Then their parents heard,
And they came running,
Bringing buckets in their hands
To hold the precious fire . . . .
We slowly doled the embers out,
Knowing their houses were
So cold.

Tamiko Yamamuro

NIGHT

We prowl through midnight streets
Searching for homeless ones,
Thinking to find them shelter.
Here and there they lie,
Wrapped in torn matting
Made of rushes.

A garbage wagon
Is a bed for one;
Pillowed upon his arm,
He snores and snores.
There from a platform made of boards
A great, broad pair of feet
Stick out into the street.

Broken umbrellas,
Tied together,
Guard the man
Who mends them,
As he sleeps
Too restlessly.
His hollow cough
Follows us through the dark.
We pass a school;
Under the jutting eaves
Two children sleep
Upon the stones . . . .

Tamiko Yamamuro

IN PRISON

WAR:

And the heavy hand
Of Thought Police
Upon our band,
Because we call ourselves an Army,
And proclaim that Christ is King!
Our possessions seized,
And papers searched;
Our soldiers persecuted;
Leaders thrown in jail.

We prisoners,
Smitten on one cheek,
Must turn the other —
Yet it gives us joy
To suffer thus for Christ.

Sometimes we find it hard
To suffer silently,
Although we know, too well,
That we must hold our peace . . . .

Even so, forgive me, Lord,
When I am tempted
To cry out in anger —
For I long to speak
Always in love.

In these dark days of weakness
I am comforted to know
Brave women long ago
Followed our Lord to Calvary,
While strong men fled.
And I remember Mary Magdalene
Who was first to greet Him
In that Easter dawn!

Surrounded by the cruel men
Who persecute us needlessly,
I think of Saul the Persecutor —
He who died a saint!
And so I fix my mind
Upon the power of God.
Then hope comes back,
Hope for our jailers
And for this poor land
        I love!

Tamiko Yamamuro

FLOOD

Day after day of ceaseless rain,
And water creeping
Into the little homes.
Under the dim street lamp
I see a woman paying tuppence
For the next day's food.

Laborers sit about the wireless
In the doss house,
Waiting news of coming weather.
When they hear
There will be rain
They groan and grumble.

We feed the hungry
Flooded out of home;
They come with boxes,
Broken bowls and pans,
And stand in line.
A woman spreads a cloth,
Saying shamefacedly
That she has pawned her pot.

"White rice! Nice rice!"
A thin boy shouts.
He must be one
Who is tired out
With leavings from cheap restaurants.
Wind shakes the tent,
But one man sits, unheedingly.
He is so glad to eat —
The rice ball in his hand
Is mixed with *meat!*

Tamiko Yamamuro

GOD'S WORD

Out of God's Word clear, living waters roll,
    And form a never-failing well of love
        Within the soul!

Takayoshi Matsuyama
(A translator of the Bible)

[55]

A NEW YEAR BRIDE

We helped to save her from the life
To which her father sold her.
And today,
This New Year's Day,
She is a bride.
A lovely bit of cloth,
All plum-strewn,
Was her parting gift to me . . . .
I cannot gaze upon those flowers enough!

Tamiko Yamamuro

CLINGING TO THEE

I fall and stumble as I grope my way
Along the path of life, unknown and hard;
But oh, that path is happiness to me
When I can cling to Thy dear hand, my Lord!
No one is left on earth who loves or tends me,
What do I seek for — I, whose eyes are blind?
It is but this — to joy in what God sends me,
His will for me to search for, and to find.
My sins through washing in the blood which cleanses,
Forever and forever are forgiven;
Casting my load on him Who loved the weary,
Steadfast and sure, I journey on toward Heaven.

*"Blind One"**

*The writer was blind, and lived alone. Each morning he prayed aloud
and sang this hymn.

[56]

Part Three

SELECTED CLASSICAL POEMS

Interpreter's Foreword

$\mathcal{B}$ECAUSE we wish this book to do its part in "bringing again love out of hatred," we present in Part Three a collection of the tiny verses known as Japanese classical poetry. We believe they will have their own appeal. Some of them were written more than a thousand years ago. They have no "message." They do not sing of faith, nor love, nor war. Delicate as "the little drop of dew dotting the tip of wayside grass," their theme is beauty in nature: the seasons, blossoms, butterflies, the chirping of insects, the moon, the pines, the snow. There is no accent, few figures of speech, no music except the liquid flowing of the language in which they were written.

Rules of composition are strict. *Tanka,* or the longer forms, are limited to thirty-one syllables. Most of the short poems in Part Two are of this type. Practically all the verses in Part Three are, however, in the shorter *hokku* (or *haiku*) form. They contain but seventeen syllables. The present writer has translated them directly from the original Japanese as found in Asataro Miyamori's exhaustive *Anthology.* Readers may be familiar with a few of the more famous selections. They have appeared in many English versions.

A Japanese has said, "Our poems are like seeds. The hearer must grow his own flowers." Depending upon none of the decorative devices usual in poetry of other languages, beauty of thought is the supreme essential. A literal translation would not be appreciated. The interpreter must feel in his heart the true meaning of the

Japanese. He must then express it in the English words
he would have used if the thought had been his own.

> *Kura yakete,*
> *Sawaru mono naki,*
> *Tsuki-mi kana!*

> Storehouse burned,
> Things-to-touch are not;
> Oh, the moon-view!

> Fire burned my storehouse,
> And my goods are gone;
> But now more clearly I can see
>   The rising moon!

Masahide
A.D. 1656-1723

PICTURES

Do you ask for a picture
Lo,
Daybreak,
And out of the haze
A moon on snow!

Michihiko
A.D. 1755-1818

Pure, and fragile and pale,
    Far and high,
Above the mist a mountain peak
    Hangs in the sky.

Kiyowara
A.D. 900-930

SWEEP OF THE TIDE

Two little boats sail side by side
    Over the sparkling bay;
But time and tide and the waves divide,
As they speed on their twinkling way;
    And they'll drift at last,
    (Oh break, my heart!)
To harbors far as the world apart.

Hochi

(An amplification)   A.D. 1118-1190

Even the Rocks of Futami
Are decked with the garlands of spring;
On the waves that ride the sweep of the tide
White sea-flowers are blossoming!

Bashō
A.D. 1644-1694

An island etched on a silver sky;
Rough waves, by a chill wind driven;
One tall sail out alone on the sea,
And the stars of the River of Heaven!

Bashō
A.D. 1644-1694

BIRD SONGS

Above white clouds I hear sweet
    voices ringing;
Be still, my heart, for oh, it is
    the skylarks singing!

Kyoroku
A.D. 1655-1715

The waving ripe fields glow with gold,
Through sunny springtime hours;
So beautiful, the little birds
Have come to see the flowers!

Bashō
A.D. 1644-1694

Birds sit and sing among the flowers,
And laugh at men, who have no time to sing!

Shōu
A. D. 1860

FLOWERS

I've not the heart to pick the violets,
Nor yet to leave them there, so small and lone.

Naojo
DATE UNKNOWN

What kind of men are these
Who try to put
A price on orchids?

Shiki
A.D. 1866-1902

This, then, the end of a dream of power,
Only a mound of grass, and a tangled flower!

Bashō
A.D. 1644-1694

NESTING

High noon;
And on the clouds above,
The sweet larks sit and sing.

Shiki
A.D. 1866-1902

The tree will soon be hewn
To earth, and fall;
The little birds go on
To build their nests,
      Because
They do not know,
Nor care at all.

Issa
A.D. 1763-1827

CHERRY BLOSSOMS

I breathe but, "Oh!"
Dumb at the loveliness of cherry flowers
      On Yoshino!

Moritake
A.D. 1472-1549

These cherry flowers
To us poor mortals given —
Could they be lovelier
If dropped from Heaven?

Issa
A.D. 1763-1827

Cherry flowers,
So wonderful
They make the warrior dismount
To gaze at them!

Issa
A.D. 1763-1827

There are no gloomy days
In cherry blossom time;
For when the sun is hid
The sweet flowers shine!

Kyohaku
DIED A.D. 1698

DISCORD

A nightingale sat singing out his heart
        one day;
The sparrows woke and heard him, and the
        sparrows flew away!

Tōrin
A.D. 1638-1719

I thrilled to hear the heavenly
        singing of the nightingale;
The oyster hawker's* raucous voice
Bawled out and broke the spell!

Yaha
A.D. 1662-1740

All day
The bird sits in his cage,
Not singing,
For he sees the butterflies!

Issa
A.D. 1763-1827

* *Beancurd seller* in the original.

BUTTERFLIES

Look! On the great bronze bell
There in the temple keep
A frail white butterfly
Lies fast asleep!

Buson
A.D. 1715-1785

I thought I saw a fallen flower
    On cold stones lie;
It fluttered, fluttered to its stem,
    A butterfly!

Moritake
A.D. 1472-1549

PROMISES

Night;
And a doorway left ajar
In the white moonbeams;
For you promised your spirit would come to me, Love,
    In my dreams!

Yakamochi
Died A.D. 785

White plum tree, where can my loved
        one be?
How the scent of your blossoms brings back
        to me
The thrill of a memory you share with me —
    But the pale spring moon is cold!

Fujiwara
A.D. 1158-1237

White of the first light snow,
    With brown sod blending;
Under its light caress
    Jonquil leaves bending!

Bashō
A.D. 1644-1694

PETALS

Perfume of plum upon the air
    Of a mountain road;
        Suddenly,
Bright on the white flower clouds,
The red sun glowed!

Bashō
A.D. 1644-1694

Nightfall;
And I all lone
Upon the moor;
So must a tree
My shelter be —
My host, a flower.

From the Noh play
TADANORI

Through an old field
My pathway led;
    Like snow
Peach petals blew and flew
Around my head.

Dakotsu
A.D. 1885

LILY AND LOTUS

Far beyond
White lilies, wild around my feet,
The smoke from Mount Asama
Drifts along the sky.

Kyokō
A.D. 1930

For lack of rain
The water must be drawn
Even from lotus ponds
To keep alive the grain!

Rakuten
A.D. 1865

The butterflies can scarcely find
A resting place among the lilies
Swaying in the wind.

Kyoshi
A.D. 1874

LISTENING AT NIGHT

I sit alone and listen
By the dim star light
To the little singing voices
Of the autumn night.

Kijō
A.D. 1870

A summer night
With breezes sweet,
And rippling waves
About a tall blue heron's feet!

Buson
A.D. 1715-1785

Some ears are tuned to catch the
          insects' songs;
And some hear only clack of
          human tongues!

Wafū
A.D. 1866

MORNING GLORIES

A homeless beggar
But he dwells among
The glorious morning glories!

Izan
A.D. 1868

Small tendrils of a morning glory to the well ropes
       cling;
Then let me go beg water from my neighbor's spring!
Chiyō Ni
A.D. 1701-1775

STEEP PATHS

He is so little, and the way is dim;
O Angel, stoop, I pray, and carry him.

Okura
A.D. 660-733

The path we have climbed has been steep and hard,
Though the two of us walked together;
How can you go on now alone, dear heart,
Through the chill of the autumn weather?

Princess Daihaku
SEVENTH CENTURY

Smiles on my lips, while quick tears blind my eyes;
Where have you wandered, Little Lad,
      Chasing dragon-flies?

Chiyō Ni
A.D. 1701-1775

INSECTS IN MY GARDEN

O little insects in my autumn garden,
    Sing you with might and main;
The cheery chirping of your merry voices
    Makes my heart young again!

Miyamori
A.D. 1938

Lightly, lightly,
Summer breezes playing,
Perched upon a blade of grass
A dragon-fly is swaying.

Bokujin
A.D. 1878

Still chirp the crickets
      Cheerfully,
Giving no sign
That they are soon to die.

Bashō
A.D. 1644-1694

FIREFLIES

The cunning fireflies
Fleeing from the chase,
Have hidden in the moon!

Ryōtō
A.D. 1660-1717

The silly little fireflies
Give their light
To guide the lads
Who race and chase them
Through the night.

Demaru
A.D. 1719-1805

A firefly
Flitted by; —
I called out
"Look!"
But lo,
I was alone.

Ryōtō
A.D. 1660-1717

The fireflies massed upon the palm fronds,
    In the dark,
        Are like bright flowers!

Buson
A.D. 1715-1783

GOLDEN MOON

Dear little one,
I would still your cry;
But the moon that you beg for
Sails too high!

Issa
A.D. 1763-1827

A band of beggars out to view
the moon;
And one was telling of his happier
days.

Kōhei
DATE UNKNOWN

Two slender stalks of black bamboo,
Holding a golden moon!

Shi-ei
A.D. 1868

NIGHT FISHERMAN

I thought my net was full of shining fish,
But when I shook it all that I had caught
    Was just the moon!

Otō
A.D. 1871

I gathered in my rod and line
Where early nightfall found me;
For there the yellow primrose bloomed
In masses all around me!

Tōyō
A.D. 1892

AUTUMN

Flying birds,
    Beware!
The maples are blazing,
    Oh, take care!

Shikō
A.D. 1644-1731

Now Autumn comes to me;
    Ah, would that I
Like maple leaves might turn
    Beautiful,
    Then die.

Shikō
A.D. 1664-1731

How can I tell you, dear,
How truly I am alone?
No flowers are left on earth,
Since you are gone!

Sōseki
A.D. 1865-1915

THE TEXT OF THIS BOOK WAS SET IN LINOTYPE FAIRFIELD,
A TYPE FACE DESIGNED BY RUDOLPH RUZICKA, ONE OF
AMERICA'S LEADING TYPE DESIGNERS. THE FORMAT IS
BY LOUISE E. JEFFERSON. THE BOOK WAS COM-
POSED AND LITHOGRAPHED BY THE LATHAM
PROCESS CORPORATION, NEW YORK, AND WAS
BOUND BY BOOK CRAFTSMEN ASSOCIATES, INC.,
NEW YORK.

•

THE ARTIST

The decorations and illustrations are by Henry Sugimoto,
California-born artist whose work has won wide recogni-
tion. Mr. Sugimoto was graduated from the California
College of Arts and Crafts with the degree of Bachelor
of Fine Arts, and later studied at the California School
of Fine Arts, the University of California, and the
Académie Colarossi in Paris. His work has been ex-
hibited at the Salon Nikka in Japan, the Salon d'Automne
and Salon Indépendant in Paris, and in many American
galleries. In 1937 he was one of sixteen representative
artists selected to exhibit at the Second National Exhi-
bition of American Art at Rockefeller Plaza in New
York. His pictures appear in the collections of museums
in the United States and France, and have been added
to many private collections.